THE ART

by the Editors of HOUSE & GARDEN

SIMON AND SCHUSTER

OF CARVING

with an introduction by JAMES A. BEARD

NEW YORK · 1963

Sketches are by

Charles B. Slackman and Edward Kasper

Photographs are by

Frank and Janet Beyda   Max Eckert   William Grigsby

Hugh McKevitt   Cyril Read Jones

FIRST PRINTING

Library of Congress Catalog Card Number: 63-19274
Manufactured in the United States of America
Printed by R. R. Heywood Company, Inc., New York

CONTENTS

FOREWORD

THE ART OF CARVING *came into being for a very personal reason. Two years ago my husband and I got into a friendly argument about the best way to carve a leg of lamb. I maintained it should be carved straight down, as you carve a ham. He was all for the slanting cut. To settle our difference, I looked for the definitive volume on carving—a Christmas present for him, I thought. But I could find nothing. Despite the great wave of gourmet gift books, the subject of carving seemed to have been completely overlooked. When I discussed this amazing omission with James A. Beard, House & Garden's food and wine consultant, we decided that full-scale recognition of the neglected art of carving was overdue. That was the genesis of House & Garden's monthly Carving Club series, for which we invited some of the world's master carvers to demonstrate their skill before the camera and explain in words their tricks and techniques. Now we have collected and printed the articles in this book—a book we believe you will want to give and to own.*

—HARRIET BURKET
Editor-in-Chief, HOUSE & GARDEN

INTRODUCTION

CARVING IS one of the more spectacular of the table arts if it is done properly. What a treat it is to watch a host or hostess with good knives, a steady hand, an understanding of anatomy and the skill to make each slice of meat fall rippling.

Centuries ago, before other refinements of the table came into being, carving was already established as a respected art. Elaborate rules governed the disposition of meat, fish and fowl—which could be touched with the hands, which not—and the royal carver cut and served using only his broad-bladed knife, with the occasional help of a spoon. He performed with astonishing virtuosity and showmanship at medieval feasts where the menu featured entire swans and peacocks, great barons of mutton or beef, and scores of small birds. Then, as in later eras, the carver was always a gentleman of good lineage, and frequently a nobleman.

Ladies carved their way onto the banquet scene when gastronomic styles changed and more manageable cuts of meat, resembling ours, began to appear on tables. (You will note, incidentally, that a section of this book is turned over to a woman who is a truly superb carver.) In Elizabethan times, for her lord's convenience the lady of the household was placed at the upper end of the table to carve and to see that important guests "above the salt" were served the choicest pieces. As the custom grew, the status of women changed from one of servitude to a position of honor. Again, the etiquette of carving was precise and was taught by especially qualified schoolmistresses and professors. The fork had come into use but was still not proper for carving. Thus, paper decorations protected a lady's delicate hand from a greasy roast. You can see the hangover from this tradition in some of today's fancier butcher shops.

Toward the close of the seventeenth century, the English adopted the "Dutch fashion"—one wonders how it could have been otherwise—of placing men and women alternately at table. With gentlemen on either side of m'lady, it was inevitable that they should assist in carving. By Victorian and Edwardian days the carving role had almost reverted to the male. It was the head of the household, usually Father, who carved, and with great ceremony. Victorian women carved also, and when they did, it was, with never a ragged edge, never too thick a slice.

A lady Bostonian published a treatise on carving in 1887 in which she encouraged more women to carve for themselves rather than to depend on their husbands and fathers. Writing with somewhat grisly good sense, she stated:

"To expect any one to carve well without any conception of the internal structure of what may be placed before him is as absurd as to expect one to amputate a limb successfully who has no knowledge of human anatomy." But then, the author prided herself on having been taught by a friend who was, in turn, tutored by a surgeon.

This same author admonished her pupils not to appear to make hard work of carving: "Avoid all scowling or contortion of the mouth if a difficult spot be touched." And a word for the guests: "Never stare at the carver. Remember you are invited to dine, not to take a lesson in carving."

Well, this brief history of carving has its point. By now it is clear than an art which once had a royal audience is getting stage fright. It isn't long before the roast is banished to the sideboard for the servant to look after, or else it is dismantled in the pantry. The behind-the-scenes approach prevails today, even in France, where the custom was introduced as *"service à la russe."*

It is all a pity. I well remember, when I was young, my mother was often the carver at our house, and it was she who began my early training. This was a time when other sons were trained by their fathers; it was considered an inseparable part of good breeding. The boys were permitted to practice when the family dined alone, and later they might be asked to assist when there were guests. What a thrilling debut that was for the youngster who had really mastered his lessons. Nowadays I know too few fathers who can carve, let alone pass on the craft to their sons. Women have become equally indifferent. Hacking is more the order of the day than carving.

Even back in 1875, a gentleman writing on the subject of the table was lamenting the same decline. "The change of fashion," he noted, "which degraded carving from the rank of the elegant accomplishments, gave the *coup de grâce* to the Beak Street Academy, where, so late as thirty years since, a lady on the eve of her marriage might acquire the art of cutting meat, in a course of twelve lessons, at a guinea a lesson, exclusive of the cost of the viands on which she operated."

Are there any brides and grooms today who do not receive a handsome carving set for a wedding present? Does either ever learn how to use it?

The art of *découpage* may never attain its former glory, and no father dissecting the holiday turkey will ever perform with the flourish of a medieval carver with his swan; but in this decade, when interest in good food continues to grow and "gourmet" has become part of the American language, it seems remarkable that this basic technique of food presentation remains neglected. We hope this volume will contribute to a new age of carvers.

—JAMES A. BEARD

KNIVES: THE CARVER'S TOOLS

THE FIRST STEP on the road to becoming a skilled carver is a knowledge and appreciation of first-rate cutlery. Though most knives today are made of stainless steel, which has the advantage of not discoloring, many carvers prefer the old-fashioned carbon steel, which takes and retains a finer cutting edge; but this is a matter of personal taste. The best knives are hollow-ground—the method used to give straight razors a keen edge. They cost more than flat- or roll-ground knives, but are well worth it. A carving knife should have a sturdy handle that enables you to get a good grip. If the handle is wood, or a similar material, it should be firmly riveted to the metal.

How many carving knives do you need? At least five different knives, of various shapes and sizes. First, a long thin slicer for ham and beef, sometimes called a *tranchelard*. This thin, supple-bladed knife, nine to fourteen inches long and about three-quarters to one inch wide, is invaluable for cutting long, wafer-thin slices of ham or for standing rib roasts. You may also use it for lamb, though a smaller, sturdier knife is better. Next, you need a knife with a wider and heavier blade, about seven inches long, and another slightly smaller. These can be used for carving leg of lamb, shoulder of veal, loin of pork and for poultry and game birds which require a knife with some delicacy, yet strong enough to cut through the bone. The smaller knife is also a great aid as a second carver for a standing rib roast or a turkey, and excellent for steaks and small pork or lamb roasts. The third type of knife you will need is a French chef's knife with a heavy triangular blade, useful for carving flat roasts and steaks. Lastly, get a boning knife with a slightly curved blade and a good grip. It is helpful for small tricky jobs and a boon in the kitchen. Buy a steel or carborundum hone and use it frequently. This will keep your knives in perfect condition. However, if you feel you are not too successful at the job, track down a good knife sharpener. Your butcher will be able to recommend one.

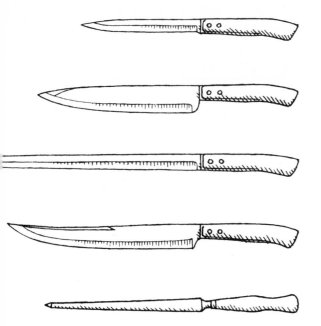

A small boning knife, with blade about 5" long, is for cutting around bones in steak or joints of fowl.

Chef's knife with heavy triangular blade, about 8" long, is good for steaks and boneless roasts.

Ham slicer has 9" to 14" blade, is used for large pieces of meat—ham, sirloin or rib roasts.

Standard roast slicer, with a sturdy blade 7" or longer, is also suitable for poultry or game.

Steel should be used, as below, to true the knife and keep the cutting edge keen and razor-sharp.

HOW TO SHARPEN A KNIFE

Hold steel in the left hand. Place the edge of the knife blade near tip of steel. Steel and blade should be at an angle of 20° (see below) so the tiny bevel at the cutting edge will be properly ground. With a quick swinging motion of right wrist and forearm, bring the knife down and across the steel, maintaining the angle, until the tip touches the bottom. Bring back to the first position on the opposite side of the steel and repeat the motion in alternating strokes. About twelve strokes should be enough. Last strokes should be very light. At no time should the side of the blade touch the steel or it will be scratched.

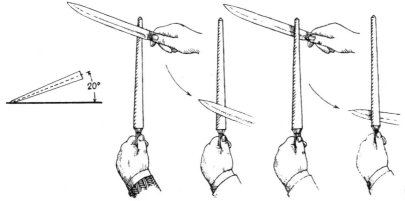

CONTINUED ▶

THE CARE AND KEEPING OF KNIVES

A good knife may not be as hard to find as a good man, but if you want to keep it good, you have to care for and about it. Guard jealously the special knives you use for carving, boning and cutting up meat and poultry. Have a second set of less efficient and less expensive knives for household help, or for your youngsters who will probably not understand the necessity of maintaining a fine edge and looking after fine steel, and who are given to seizing the nearest knife to slice through the string on a package. They will be just as happy with "Brand X" knives, and you can then rest assured that *your* blades will be in mint condition when you need them.

GIVE A KNIFE A GOOD HOME

Crowded drawers are death on blades; they soon become blunted or nicked through constant rubbing against hard objects. If you are obliged to keep knives in a drawer, have it slotted so the knives are separated from each other and can be removed easily. Unquestionably, the place to store your knives is in a unit designed to keep them handy and uncrowded. There are some workmanlike versions on the market, or, if you don't find what you are looking for, it is a relatively simple matter to build what you want. A knife-storage unit can be portable or stationary, and decorative as well as functional. A magnetic knife rack that attaches to a wall or

Magnetic steel knife rack can be easily attached to any wall, keeps knives within easy reach.

cabinet and holds the blades flat against the magnetic steel strips is inexpensive and perfectly adequate. However, if you intend to use it for your carving knives, make sure that the magnet is really strong enough to hold the weight of a big carving knife. Some cutlery manufacturers sell slotted wood racks that can be used freestanding or mounted on the wall. The only drawback is that they are constructed to take the manufacturers' own knives and may not be scaled to your own diverse collection.

It is not hard to construct a simple rack with slots for knives; a slightly more ambitious storage unit, still within the skill of the amateur, is a case made of three-quarter-inch-thick pine boards with an acrylic plastic front that slides out at one side for cleaning (see sketch). This can be free-standing or attached to the wall, and protects the knives and at the same time keeps them at hand and in view. A really professional kind of storage, seen in the sketch below, is a chopping-block table with slots at the side to hold the knives.

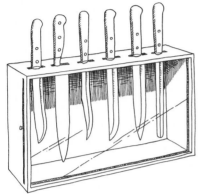

Slotted knife rack is an easy job for the home craftsman. The front is clear acrylic plastic.

For experts who use a chopping-block table, an open knife rack along one side is the best solution.

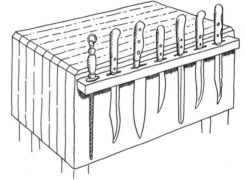

KEEP KNIVES CLEAN AND STAIN-FREE

Just as crowded drawers blunt knives, so do crowded sinks. Never dump your knives in a sink or dishpan with other cutlery and dishes; this not only harms the blade but the immersion weakens the bond between blade and handle (and also you run the risk of getting cut when you plunge your hands in the water). The best way to keep a knife clean is to wipe it with a damp or wet sponge after each use and promptly dry it. If you make a habit of doing this, you shouldn't have any staining problem, even with non-stainless steel knives. Non-stainless steel will darken with use—an honorable mark in the eyes of most carvers. If stains do appear on your blades, clean them with steel wool and coarse salt (you may find it necessary to add a little vinegar to the salt). Careful storage, prompt cleaning, and constant use of your steel or carborundum, plus an occasional professional sharpening, will keep your knives in prime condition for many years. Remember that good tools, properly cared for and properly used, are the first essentials if you want to become a really expert, confident carver.

MEAT
AND
POULTRY

HOW TO CARVE
HAM

PROPER CARVING makes the meal, according to André Surmain, whose small select restaurant, Lutèce, has become a haven for New Yorkers seeking superbly prepared and served French food. Here Mr. Surmain demonstrates the French style of carving a ham in paper-thin slices, recommended for cold ham or Virginia hams.

THE FRENCH STYLE

1 *Arrange the ham on a platter with the top facing up. Cut straight down to the bone near the shank end.*

2 *Make a second, slanting cut rather higher up to connect with the first cut. Remove and discard this wedge, which will consist of excess fat.*

3 *Start slicing at a 30-degree angle to the bone, keeping the slices very thin and even.*

4 *Remove the slices to a plate as they are carved. Continue carving the ham until about one third of it is sliced.*

5 *Now carve from one side to the middle in thin half-slices.*

6 *Repeat this procedure on the other side, alternating to keep the ham even.*

HOW TO CARVE
PORK

PORK SHOULD always be well done, and it is wonderfully succulent when properly roasted. A popular roast is the loin, which you can carve into sturdy chops, as demonstrated by Pancho Velez, executive chef of Detroit's London Chop House, seen below with one of the co-owners, Lester Gruber. Or carve thin chops plus boneless slices from between the ribs. Another roast is a leg of pork, or fresh ham.

A PORK LOIN ROAST

1 *Stand the roast upright on the end from which the backbone (chine) has been removed to make carving easier. Hold the roast steady with a fork.*

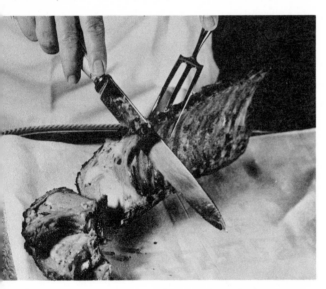

2 *Make the cut between the ribs. Carve downward, following the line of the ribs. For a thin chop, cut near the rib bone, leaving the meat between.*

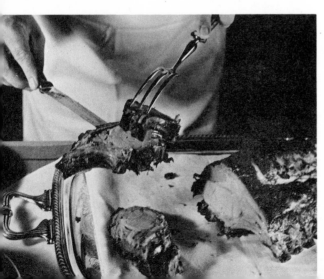

3 *Pick up the chops with the knife and fork and remove them to a plate. Serve the chops with applesauce flavored with freshly grated horseradish.*

A FRESH HAM

Fresh ham, less widely available than the smoked and cured variety, makes a delicious roast with a delicate texture. You can occasionally order fresh ham with the skin on—during roasting it crisps to tasty crackling. Fresh hams range from eight to twenty pounds, and the larger, more mature hams are best. If you do not want a big ham, you can buy a half. The carving technique for a fresh roasted ham is basically the same as that for a smoked and cured ham.

1 *Hold the ham firmly on a spiked board or cut a piece from the bottom to make a flat base. Cut a small wedge from the shank end.*

2 *Starting at the shank end, carve straight down toward the leg bone, cutting the meat in fairly thin, delicate slices.*

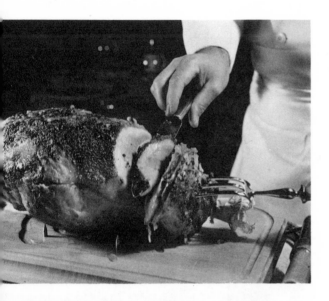

3 *As each slice is cut, push it back toward the shank end with the knife blade so as not to impede carving.*

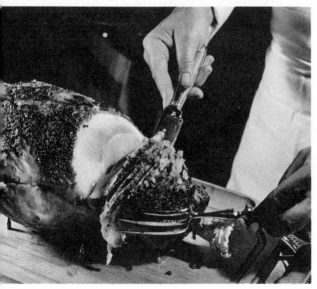

4 *When enough slices are cut, run the knife underneath them at right angles to the slices, releasing them from the bone. After this side is carved, turn the ham over and repeat the same procedure on the other side.*

HOW TO CARVE
A SUCKLING PIG

SUCKLING PIG, a delicacy well known in Spain and Latin America, has an ardent if limited following here. Lloyd Bryan, of Napa, California, a master of outdoor hostmanship, recommends suckling pig for a large summer barbecue. "Pig is a very rich beast," says Mr. Bryan, "and should not be served too often, but it is wonderfully spectacular." His special way of cooking the pig slowly on an enclosed grill results in a rich mahogany skin and succulent flesh that yields to the knife. Frequently Mr. Bryan cooks the pig on a plywood plank which later, camouflaged by leaves and flowers, acts as platter and carving board.

1 *Insert the point
of the knife, cutting edge up,
under the skin of the pig
near the tail.
Cut upward in a straight line
from the tail to the neck.*

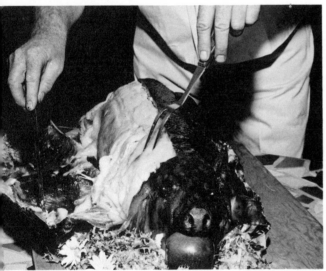

2 *Push the skin
to one side with the knife;
it should fall away.*

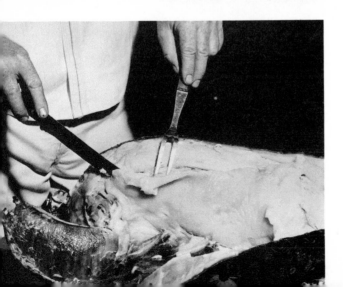

3 *With the knife,
slice off as much of
the covering layer of
fat as possible,
in order to expose the
meat underneath.*

CONTINUED ▶

A SUCKLING PIG

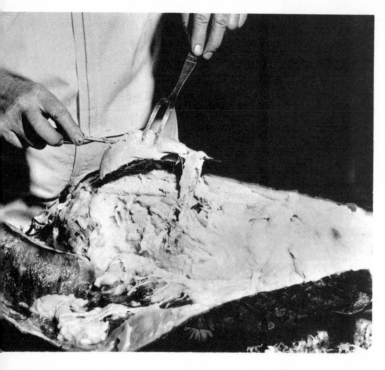

4 *Carve the meatiest part of the pig (the ham) first. As you would with chicken, slice with, not against, the grain.*

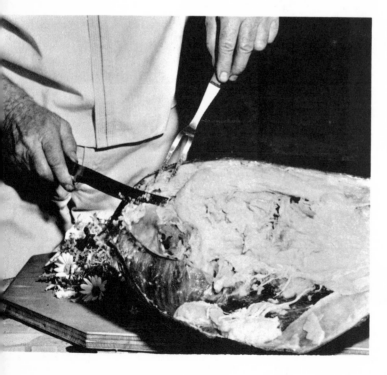

5 *Carve the ham into individual portions and arrange them on plates.*

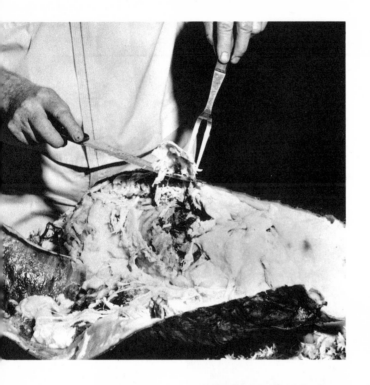

6 *Separate the ribs with a spoon, and then remove them with the knife and fork. Serve the meat as requested in individual servings.*

7 *After the ribs are removed, spoon the dressing from the cavity and serve it. Lastly, carve and serve the meat from the shoulder.*

HOW TO CARVE
ROAST BEEF

TO MANY AMERICANS, meat is synonymous with beef, and a roast with roast beef. The finest of our beef roasts is undoubtedly the standing rib roast, magnificent in both appearance and flavor. Calculate around one pound per serving and buy at least a three-rib roast. For a party you may need a five- or even seven-rib roast, if your oven can accommodate it. Carving is easier if you have the chine bone (backbone) removed by the butcher and the rib bones cut short. Usually a rib roast is carved in slices, but for hearty eaters you might like to serve a whole rib, an inch thick. Mr. Jan Mitchell, genial owner of Luchow's restaurant in New York, shows you how to carve a standing rib roast.

A STANDING RIB ROAST

1 *Arrange the meat on a platter with the largest end down to form a solid base. For a whole rib serving, cut under the first rib, near the bone, slicing the meat from the rib tip inward.*

2 *To lift the whole rib neatly, pick it up with the knife underneath and hold it steady with the fork.*

3 *Carve individual slices of desired thickness until you come to the second rib. With the tip of the knife, cut along the rib bone to loosen the meat from the bone.*

4 *Arrange the individual servings on plates, or transfer them from the serving platter after the roast is carved.*

A SIRLOIN ROAST

This is the famous "roast beef of old England" and a specialty of Simpson's in the Strand, London. A whole sirloin roast, though more expensive than a rib roast, is economical because there is less waste in bone and fat. The flavor is superb. Here Mr. Frank Wood, head carver at Simpson's, demonstrates how a good knife, know-how and confidence make a master carver.

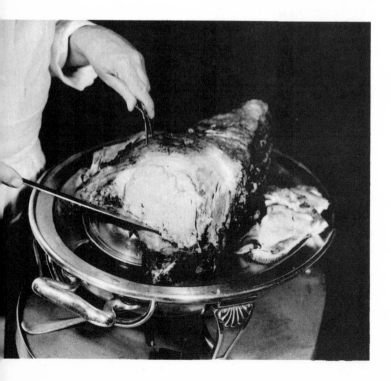

1 *Starting at the larger end of the roast, remove a piece from the end. With the point of the knife, cut under the piece to remove it from the bone.*

2 *With the point of the knife, remove the fat and gristle from the chine of beef.*

3 *Carve in thin slices from the fat side at an angle to the bone. Hold the carving knife with the thumb against the handle and the forefinger pressed against the back of the blade. This grip gives the greatest control while carving.*

HOW TO CARVE
AND GARNISH A
FILLET OF BEEF

A FILLET, or whole boneless beef tenderloin, is an elegant roast for a dinner party. On the face of it, a fillet would seem to present no carving problem, but the tenderness of its texture and the fact that it should always be served juicily rare require delicacy in handling and slicing. The expert's way with a fillet is capably demonstrated here by Guido Bocchiola, co-owner of New York's L'Aiglon restaurant. A fillet, although delicious, is not a showy roast, and it profits from a surrounding garnish of colorful vegetables.

1 *Place the fillet on a board. Hold it in place with the back of the fork; do not pierce it with the tines. Cut a slice from the wide end of the fillet.*

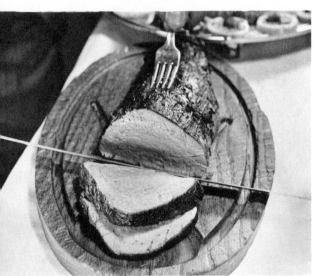

2 *Working a long, sharp slicer smoothly back and forth straight across the meat, cut slices three quarters of an inch to one inch thick.*

3 *Keep the blade straight and draw it toward you as you cut downward. The middle slices will be the rarest.*

CONTINUED ▶

GARNISHING

A GARNISH not only decorates the platter but also provides small portions of such appropriate vegetables as string beans, broccoli, white asparagus, baby carrots, tomatoes, peas, mushrooms on artichoke bottoms. Lemon slices are for show.

Garnishes, according to *Larousse Gastronomique*, can be many, varied, and complicated. For simple meals at home, you are better advised to keep the garnishes simple, limited, and in small shapes and quantities suitable for individual servings. Try to shape or supplement the vegetables in ways that show off their contours and colors. An ordinary mushroom cap becomes special when fluted (1). Use a lemon stripper to remove a thin layer of peel in a series of curving cuts around the cap. Etch small stars on the tops with a sharp knife. Choose firm, white, not-too-large mushroom caps for fluting. A little potato nest (2) holds tiny new potatoes, potato balls, or *pommes soufflées*. Waffle-slice old potatoes (or shred them in julienne strips), dry well, and line the larger basket of a bird's-nest fryer (3) with them. Press the smaller basket on top to hold the potatoes in place, and deep-fry them in fat. Drain well on paper towels before using. A chef's trick for giving form and finesse to puréed vegetables or duchess potato mixture is piping. For a swirly pyramid (4), use a pastry bag with a star tube. You can pipe the mixture straight onto the platter or onto artichoke bottoms. A plain broiled tomato looks and tastes better with a topping of grated cheese and seasoned bread crumbs (5). A canned artichoke bottom (6) and a little pastry case (7) make handy containers for small, slippery vegetables such as peas, baby carrots, pearl onions, and asparagus tips.

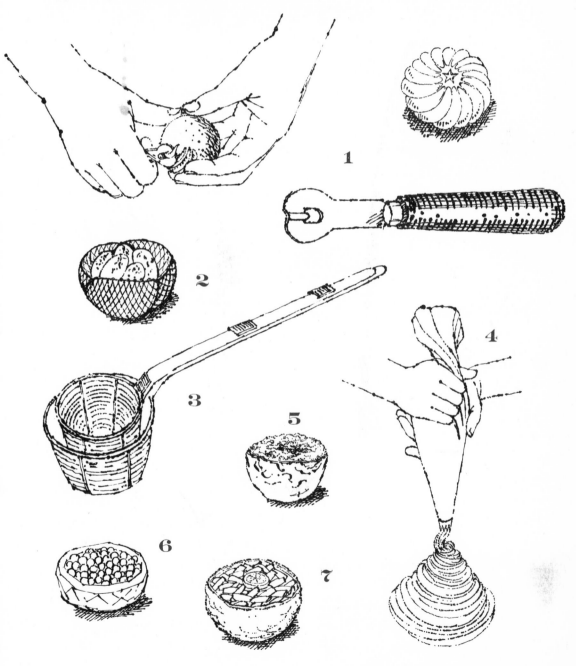

HOW TO CARVE
STEAK

SUMMER OR WINTER, outdoors and indoors, steak rates as America's favorite meat. Many people prefer the robust steaks such as porterhouse and sirloin, which taste best if cut at least two inches thick, broiled quickly and then served in manageable portions. Here, James A. Beard shows how to carve a porterhouse and a flank steak for London broil. Unlike roasts, steaks are carved *with* the grain of the meat, as the fibers are tender and short. Although a board is recommended for carving, a stainless steel platter, heated to sizzling to keep steak hot, may be more attractive.

A PORTERHOUSE STEAK

1 *With a small, sharp boning knife, start at the top of the T-shaped bone and cut down and around it. Steady the steak with a two-pronged fork.*

2 *Start at the top of the bone on the second side and cut around it. Lift out the bone and discard it.*

3 *Cut off the tail or flank end of the steak. Then, take a steak carver, hold it on a diagonal, and slice the fillet (tenderloin) section thickly.*

4 *Carve the larger loin section in the same way. Trim off the fat from the side. Put a piece of fillet and a piece of loin on each plate.*

5 *If additional servings are needed, slice the tail end.*

A FLANK STEAK

Flank steak, the economical cut used for London broil, is boneless and fat-free, but has a coarser grain than more expensive steaks. It should always be broiled rare and sliced very thin. Properly carved, a flank steak yields four to five servings. As London broil is carved in long narrow strips, you will need a long knife with a thin, sharp, flexible blade for slicing the meat.

1 *Hold the flank steak firmly on a carving board with a two-pronged carving fork. Start cutting at the small end of the flank steak.*

2 *Holding the knife blade at an angle almost parallel to the board, cut off the first slice.*

3 *Continue carving at the same angle, cutting with the grain of the meat and slicing very thin.*

4 *With the knife and fork, transfer the slices to serving plates—four to six slices per person, depending on guests' appetites and the rest of the menu.*

HOW TO CARVE
LAMB

LAMB IS a delicate and flavorful meat that affords many different types of roasts, but it often presents a problem in carving. The important thing when carving lamb is to understand the bone structure of the roast and slice it accordingly. Here Mr. Fred Decré of the Caravelle Restaurant in New York shows you the correct way to deal with a rack, saddle, and leg of lamb. Simplest to carve is the rack— a single rack of rib chops which has only to be cut into individual portions. A crown roast, the double rack tied in the form of a crown, is also carved into single chops. The saddle, a more complex cut consisting of the double loin and tenderloin, is carved in long strips on each side parallel to the spinal column. The technique for carving a leg of lamb is explained on page 42.

A RACK OF LAMB

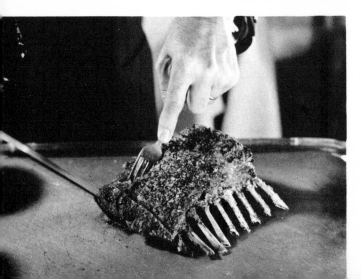

1 *Arrange the rack of rib chops on the platter with the Frenched (scraped) bone tips pointed away from the carver.*

2 *Make the first cut at the top where the chops are joined.*

3 *Separate the chops by carving between the rib bones.*

4 *Pick up the chop on the flat of the knife, holding it firmly with the carving fork, and transfer it to a plate.*

A SADDLE OF LAMB

1 *Arrange the saddle, bone side down, on a carving board. Slice off the layer of fat on the top of the saddle by cutting parallel to the meat.*

2 *With a turn of the knife, remove the layer of fat, which can be discarded.*

3 *Carve the saddle down toward the bone with the knife parallel to the spinal column. Cut the meat into thin, even, lengthwise slices.*

4 *Transfer the slices to a plate; add gravy and vegetables.*

A LEG OF LAMB

A perfectly cooked and carved leg of lamb is an asset to any menu. Although the leg is often carved down toward the bone, like a ham, the following method of slicing across the top is better from the viewpoint of appearance and flavor. You may buy a whole leg or short leg (with sirloin portion removed) as shown in the diagram. A whole leg will be easier to carve if tail and pelvic bone are removed.

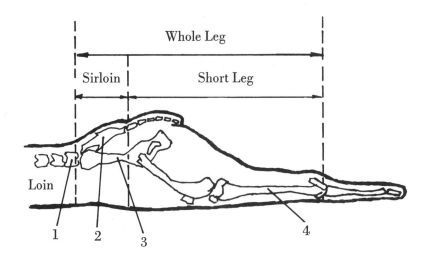

1. Chine bone   3. Pelvic bone
2. Tail   4. Shank bone

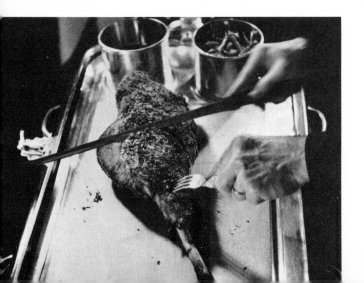

1 *Arrange the leg of lamb on a platter, bone side down, with the exposed tip of the shank pointed to the left of the carver.*

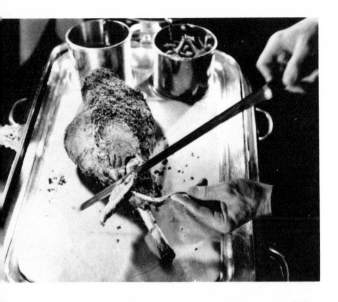

2 *With a long, flexible slicer, start carving a third of the way down the leg and cut a small slice from the top.*

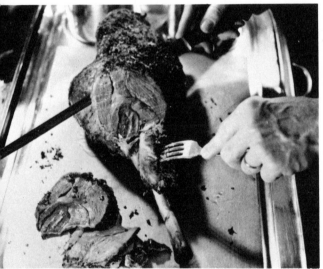

3 *Continue carving across the top of the leg with the grain of the meat. After removing the top slices, carve the sides in long slices.*

4 *Transfer the slices to a plate for individual serving. Garnish with vegetables.*

HOW TO CARVE
VEAL

TO MOST PEOPLE, veal calls up visions of chops and scaloppine, seldom a roast. Yet a veal roast, as the French have proved, can be a flavorful and delicious feast, especially in spring, when this delicate meat seems particularly suited to lighter menus. Veal's melting tenderness lends itself to different types of carving. A saddle can be carved into scallops or fillets. Or you may carve it as you would a saddle of lamb (see page 40), slicing the meat in long, thin, even strips on each side, parallel to the spine. Should you want a smaller roast, buy a rack of veal—half the saddle— and carve it into individual chops, like a rack of lamb.

Here the maître d'hôtel of M. Jean Rouhette's Le Berkeley Restaurant in Paris demonstrates a favored French method of carving saddle of veal: cutting it into fillets one inch thick. (If you prefer, this can be done in the kitchen, the meat reassembled and then taken apart when served at the table.) In the classic manner, the roast is garnished with a colorful selection of cooked vegetables temptingly arranged. More than mere decoration, the vegetables make an easy-to-serve accompaniment to the meat. For an even more elegant roast, you might have the saddle boned and stuffed with kidneys (this is called a *rognonnade*), which should be carved in round slices.

A SADDLE OF VEAL

1 *Hold the veal firmly with a fork pressed against the backbone. With a sturdy knife (here, a triangular-bladed chef's knife), slice all the way down on one side of the bone.*

2 *To carve a scallop or fillet, slice downward toward the rib bones, cutting a piece about one inch thick. Angle the knife so that the meat is sliced on a slight diagonal.*

3 *Cut all around the bone at the bottom of the scallop to release the meat. Hold the meat with the fork, slide the blade of the knife under it, and transfer it to a serving plate.*

4 *Arrange a variety of garnishing vegetables on the plate with the veal: peas in an artichoke bottom, green beans, baby carrots, cauliflower, and a skinned tomato.*

HOW TO CARVE
TURKEY

THE ROLE of family carver, once an exclusively male prerogative, is now frequently left in the hands of the lady of the house. Believing that in carving knowledge counts more than brute strength, we asked Mrs. William B. Lewis, of Riverdale, New York, an accomplished hostess who readily admits that her father taught her all she knows about carving, to show a woman's way with the holiday bird.

1 *Arrange the turkey on a platter with the drumsticks pointing to the carver's right. Cut down between the thigh and the body.*

2 *Push the leg away
from the body with the fork,
and, with the tip
of the carving knife,
sever the leg from the body
at the joint.*

3 *Remove the leg to
a serving platter or plate,
and cut it in two at the
second joint,
separating the thigh from
the drumstick.*

4 *For individual servings
of dark meat,
slice the drumstick downward
into neat pieces.
Also slice the thigh section.*

CONTINUED ▶

5 *Next, remove the wing. Press the wing tip down with the fork to reveal the joint, and sever the wing from the body with the tip of the knife.*

6 *Cut through the base of the breast horizontally so that the breast meat will fall away easily when it is sliced down.*

7 *Carve down the breast on an angle in thin slices. Continue until you reach the wide part of the breast.*

8 *Carve,
still on an angle, from the
front and back ends of the
breast alternately
so that the slices are not
too large.*

9 *Spoon stuffing
from the cavity onto the
serving platter with
the meat.*

10 *Carve the second side
of the turkey in the same way
as the first.*

HOW TO CARVE
CHICKEN

THE APPARENTLY simple matter of carving a chicken can be a minor masterpiece or a doleful disaster. The importance of correct carving, from the standpoint of both esthetics and edibility, is never underestimated in restaurants where the highest standards of cuisine are rigorously maintained. Here Albert Stockli, executive chef of Restaurant Associates, demonstrates at New York's famous Four Seasons restaurant the proper technique for carving a chicken into individual portions in the kitchen, while on page 53 one of the captains presents the niceties of table *découpage*. You'll notice that a carving knife and fork do the job in the kitchen, but at the table a smaller fork in the left hand deftly pulls the meat away as the knife loosens skin and flesh. Whether the carving is done in the kitchen or at the table, the portions are attractively arranged on the plate, joints severed to make eating easier, and a sauce added to enhance appearance and taste.

1 *As Chef Stockli demonstrates, arrange the chicken, breast up, on a carving board. Sever the skin between the leg and the body, and push the leg to the side with the knife to reveal the joint.*

2 *Slice through the cartilage between the bones of the lower joint. Remove the leg. Repeat the procedure with the other leg.*

3 *Carve the breast meat from the bone, cutting as close to the bone as possible to get the full thickness of the breast.*

4 *Press the meat to the side and continue cutting until the wing is also separated from the body. Remove the breast and wing in one piece (this section is sometimes called a suprême).*

CONTINUED ▶

5 *Repeat the procedure on the other side of the chicken. You now have two legs and two breast-and-wing sections.*

6 *Remove the leg to a plate and cut through the cartilage connecting the thigh and the drumstick.*

7 *Place the suprême on a plate and, if you wish, cut the wing from the breast meat.*

8 *Spoon over the chicken only as much sauce as is needed to give a light coating. Serve the rest in a sauceboat.*

1 *To follow the example of a captain at the Four Seasons, place the chicken on its side, with its legs pointing to the carver's left.*

2 *Spear one leg with the fork. While cutting against the body with the knife, pull the leg away with the fork. Cut off the leg and remove it.*

3 *Loosen the wing joint with the knife, and cut along the breastbone while pulling the wing off with the left hand. Use the point of the knife to detach the meat from the breastbone.*

4 *Turn the chicken over and remove the other leg.*

CONTINUED ▶

5 *Follow the same procedure to remove the second breast-wing section.*

6 *Place a leg on a plate and cut through the cartilage between the thigh and the drumstick.*

7 *Arrange the suprême at the side of the leg. Coat all the pieces with sauce.*

HOW TO CARVE
DUCK
AND GOOSE

A SUCCULENT duck or goose makes a fine departure from the usual chicken. Both should be roasted slowly on a rack or spit to draw out the fat. A three-and-one-half- to four-pound duck will serve two to four, depending on menu and appetites. A small seven- to eight-pound goose serves six to eight (this size, sometimes called a junior goose, is perfect for dinner parties, and don't count on any leftovers). Duck yields more servings if, instead of being carved in the standard manner, the meat is pulled away from the bone, a restaurant technique demonstrated here by Fred Rupprecht, executive chef of New York's Forum of the Twelve Caesars. The loosened meat can then be trimmed and halved or cut into neat, easy-to-eat serving pieces.

CONTINUED ▶

1 *With the knife, sever the skin where the leg joins the body.*

2 *Turn the duck on its side and hold it firmly with the fork placed in the cavity. With a second fork, pull the leg away from the body.*

3 *Cut through the connecting tissue at the joint. Put the leg on the carving board and cut it in two at the second joint. Arrange it on a plate.*

4 *Halve the breast by slicing downward from the neck to the tail, cutting through the bone at both ends with the knife.*

5 *Again hold the duck firmly with the fork in the cavity. With a second fork, pull off half the breast and the wing in one piece.*

6 *Turn the breast over and remove the rib bones, pulling them away from the meat. Halve or slice the breast for serving.*

A GOOSE

As goose is a larger, meatier bird than duck, the carving procedure differs slightly. Never put the fork in the breast, always in the cavity or underside of the bird.

1 *Tilt the goose on its side, holding it underneath firmly with a fork. Cut completely around the leg to loosen the meat.*

2 *Remove a section at the neck end of the goose by cutting straight across, making it easier to carve the breast.*

3 *With a long-bladed, flexible slicer, carve the breast the long way, cutting downward in thin, even slices.*

4 *With a second fork, pull the leg back and away from the body, and cut through the connecting tissue at the joint with the knife.*

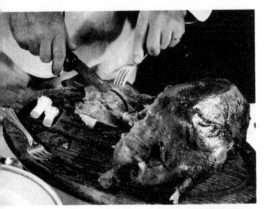

5 *Lay the leg on the carving board. Carve the meat in neat slices.*

6 *Reassemble the slices in the shape of the leg on the serving plate.*

HOW TO CARVE
PHEASANT
AND PARTRIDGE

NOW THAT pheasant and partridge are no longer exclusively the spoils of the hunter, but are raised extensively for the general market, many people elect to serve them at dinner parties. John G. Martin, chairman of Heublein Inc., who has the advantage of actually raising pheasant, chukar partridge and quail on his Connecticut game farm, is a past master in the art of carving game birds, as he shows here.

A PHEASANT

1 *Lay the pheasant on its back on the carving board. Hold the bird firm with the carving fork and sever one wing from the body.*

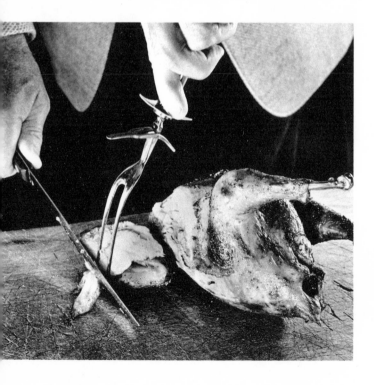

2 *Trim off and discard the bony tip from the severed wing.*

CONTINUED ▶

PHEASANT

3 *Turn the bird around so that the drumsticks point toward the carver, and cut downward to separate the leg from the body.*

4 *Press the leg back with the knife, and cut through at the joint.*

5 *Sever the thigh from the drumstick by cutting at the second joint. Remove and disjoint the second leg and wing in the same way.*

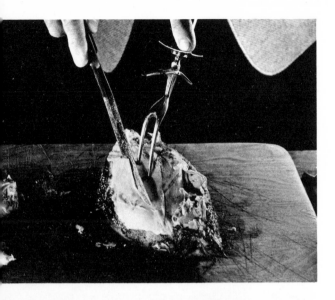

6 *Next, turn the bird over so that it lies breast down. Carve down toward the breastbone, the full length of the breast.*

7 *Carve the other breast in the same way. (Although unconventional, this method of carving from the broad side of the meat is easier.)*

8 *Allot each plate both dark and light meat. A good accompaniment is a green pepper stuffed with wild rice. A pheasant will yield meat for two to four.*

A CHUKAR PARTRIDGE

ALTHOUGH YOU can count on a pheasant serving two to four, according to size, the smaller partridge is usually considered enough at most for two—or an ample serving for one. These birds are not so much carved as split in two. However, there is a trick to splitting them neatly and effortlessly, as you can see in the following pictures.

1 *Lay the partridge breast down on the carving board. Starting at the tail, make the initial cut to the left of the breastbone.*

2 *Cut from the tail
to the head, keeping
to the left of the bone.*

3 *When the neck
is reached, sever
it with the tip of the
knife. Serve
the two halves or one
half to each person,
as you wish.*

SEAFOOD

HOW TO FILLET
SOLE AND
SALMON

FILLETING IS to fish what carving is to meat and poultry—a means of removing the flesh from the bone and serving it in manageable, easy-to-eat portions. There the resemblance ends, for the delicacy of fish requires equal delicacy of technique and tools. A spoon, fork and blunt-edged fish knife take the place of a carving set. Although much fish today is sold already boned, certain fish should be cooked whole and filleted at the table, so that the shape, texture and flavor are retained. Two good examples are a whole sole cooked *meunière* style, or broiled, fried or poached, and a whole salmon. To demonstrate the fine art of filleting at the table, we enlisted the skillful services of the manager of Prunier's in London, a restaurant that has long been synonymous in both England and France with the highest traditions of cooking and serving fish.

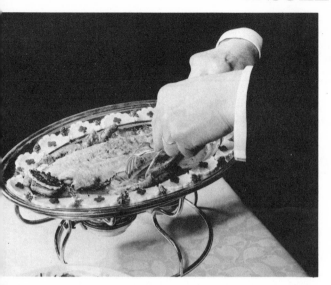

1 *Scrape away the small bones at the side of the fish with the rounded back of a spoon held in the right hand. Hold the fish with a fork.*

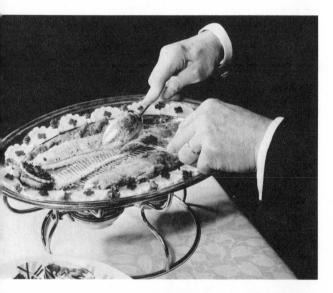

2 *With the bones at both sides of the sole removed, separate the fillets from the backbone with the spoon and the fork.*

3 *Push the fillet away from the bone with the edge of the spoon. Work from top to bottom, holding the bone firm with the fork.*

CONTINUED ▶

4 *Lift out the backbone in one piece and lay it at the side of the dish.*

5 *To serve the sole, lift the top and bottom fillets from each side with the spoon and the fork. Reshape the fillets on the serving plate.*

6 *For sole meunière, spoon the hot cooking butter over the fillets; top with parsley-sprinkled lemon slice.*

A COLD SALMON

1 *With a fish knife, make a cut down the center of the salmon as long as the piece you want to serve, and then cut around the head, if it has been left on.*

2 *Make a cut of similar length down the side of the salmon.*

3 *Cut across the top at a slight angle to release the section.*

CONTINUED ▶

COLD SALMON

4 *Slide the knife underneath the salmon section and lift it away from the bone, keeping it steady with a spoon and a fork.*

5 *Arrange the salmon on a plate. Make similar cuts on the second side and proceed as before. Continue down the length of the salmon.*

HOW TO OPEN
OYSTERS

MANY HOSTS and hostesses just give up the idea of serving oysters at home because they don't know how to open them. This is a pity, since oysters on the half shell make a gala beginning for any meal. There is a trick to opening them, and you do need a special oyster knife. The trick is relatively simple to learn, but we advise a little practice before the guests arrive. Once you get the hang of it, however, you will soon be as proficient as those wizards you have watched so enviously in oyster bars.

1 *Hold the oyster firmly, protecting your hand with several thicknesses of cloth. Insert the oyster knife in the back of the oyster to break the vacuum.*

CONTINUED ▶

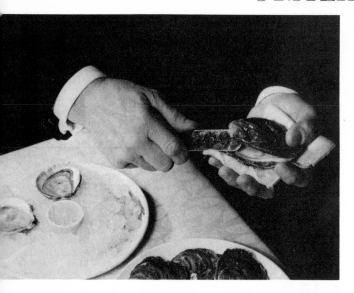

2 *Turn the knife sideways, pushing upward to separate the shells. Remove and discard the top shell.*

3 *Arrange the half shells on cracked ice. To remove the oyster cleanly from the shell, start at the side. Slide the edge of a seafood fork around and under the oyster.*

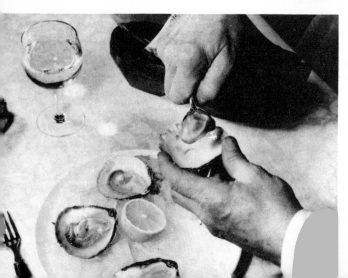

4 *Scoop up the oyster. It should come away completely.*

HOW TO DISMEMBER
A LOBSTER

IT PAYS to master the technique of killing a lobster, as even the short delay between market and pot can spoil the meat. If you are squeamish, bear in mind that the nervous system of a lobster is considerably more rudimentary than yours and that a well-placed knife or a pot of boiling water are immediate in their effect. An instant of courage and the deed is done. Here, Dione Lucas, the well-known expert cook and teacher, shows you how.

A LIVE LOBSTER

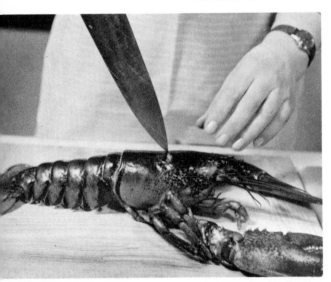

1 *Plunge the point of a heavy knife into the cross where the head and body shells meet.*

2 *Hold the lobster firmly behind the eyes. Cut down the back from the head to the tail. Turn the lobster over and split it through the head.*

CONTINUED ▶

LIVE LOBSTER

3 *Remove and discard the sac behind the eyes.*

4 *Remove and discard the intestinal vein.*

5 *Remove and reserve the green liver and, if there is any, the coral.*

6 *With heavy shears, cut off the large claws where they join the body.*

A BOILED LOBSTER

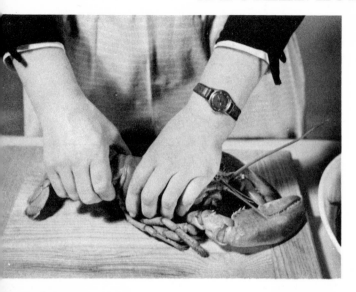

1 *Separate the tail section from the head by breaking the lobster apart with your hands.*

2 *Cut down each side of the thin under part of the tail with shears.*

3 *Remove the tail meat in one unbroken piece, ready for slicing.*

4 *With shears, cut off the big claws, and then cut these again at the second joint.*

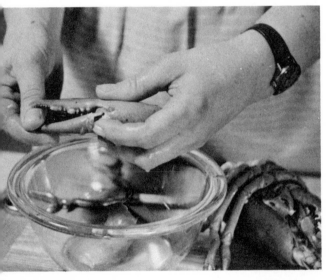

5 *Push the small claw shell behind the large one to. remove it without breaking the meat.*

6 *Cut the edges of the large claw shell and remove the meat. Do the same with the claw joints.*